The Unexpected Journey

Trusting God Through the Grieving Process

Ronald Hardy, Sr.

renownpublishing

Copyright © 2021 by **Ronald Hardy, Sr.**

All rights reserved. No part of this publication may be reproduced, distributed, or transmitted in any form or by any means, without prior written permission.

All Scripture quotations are taken from the King James Bible (KJV). Accessed on Bible Gateway. www.BibleGateway.com.

Renown Publishing
www.renownpublishing.com

The Unexpected Journey / Ronald Hardy, Sr.
ISBN-13: 978-1-952602-49-8

My relationship with Bishop Ronald and Robbin Hardy Sr. goes back many years. I have seen them be used by God to bless many lives over the years in so many ways. [From] times of our personal fellowship together [as well], I have such a fondness and respect for them.

The events that led to the writing of *The Unexpected Journey* are heartfelt and challenging, to say the least. I'm proud of the response of Bishop Hardy, that in the midst of his own pain and loss, he is used of God to minister God's love and care to others.

Not only does the book detail the final days of a great woman of God on this earth, but also the power of family, faith, and the Holy Spirit to take pain and turn it into power to minster. Bishop [Hardy]'s journey will help so many others in the times in which we live. Of course, it is not a journey that was requested, but now that he has embarked upon it, the grace of God is using it in a powerful way to heal and to help with the grief process.

I highly recommend the book and the faith of God attached to it. Bishop Hardy reveals how, through faith, you are not on your journey alone.

Bishop Raymond W Johnson
Founder and Pastor of Living Faith Christian Center
Presiding Bishop of M.O.V.E. Fellowship

Many of us can put a face on the dreaded COVID-19 virus because we have lost family, friends, co-workers, neighbors, or church members to this virus. While we have celebrated the survivors, we in too many instances have personally grieved and mourned with others over the deaths.

I have had the privilege of knowing Bishop Ronald and Prophetess Robbin Hardy for decades. They have been a part of the fabric of the Baton Rouge community.

The loss of Robbin Hardy was a tear in the fabric of our community. Sister Hardy not only lived out her faith at her church, but she [also] put her faith into action by serving her community through the Girls Enrichment Mentorship Services that she founded. She touched hundreds of lives.

In his book, *The Unexpected Journey,* Bishop Ronald Hardy turns his pain into purpose. He chronicles his personal journey of losing his wife of thirty-eight years to the coronavirus. Yet, he also helps the reader understand the reality of grief and how to process grief and loss from a biblical perspective.

I had the privilege of sitting in on one of Bishop Hardy's grief workshops. I was enlightened and empowered by the session, just as you will be when you read *The Unexpected Journey.*

Sharon Weston Broome
Mayor-President
Baton Rouge/EBR Parish

My friendship with Bishop Ronald Hardy, Sr. and his late wife, Robbin, began with an interview for my magazine, laying the foundation for our ministries' kinship. Later, while filming an episode for the *Life On Purpose* television series, only God knew COVID-19 lurked around the corner. Because of it, Robbin would soon be ushered into her heavenly home. Bishop Hardy wrote *The Unexpected Journey* to help readers navigate the devastating pain of such loss, by writing about encountering the promises of God. This book invites you into the Bishop's [healing] process, showing you how pain can become your purpose.

Beth Townsend
Founder/TV Host of "Life on Purpose"

We are all trying to make sense of life. The pandemic has made life for so many even more difficult to understand, as we have lost so many. In *The Unexpected Journey*, Bishop Ronald Hardy, Sr. has taken his experience and his journey to forge a path for all of us to see how we might not only deal with tragedy but [also] find ways to make ourselves and our world a better place.

I knew Robbin Hardy, and to know her was to experience God's love. She served our school district and our students through a mentoring program. I was hospitalized at the same time as Robbin was sick with COVID-19. It was difficult to see her succumb to the illness, yet amazing to watch her family deal with their grief through faith, trust, love, and hope.

This book will serve all of us well as 2020 and the ensuing pandemic have left us wanting change, revival, and hope. The endearing legacy of Robbin Hardy is carried through in the message of this book: that God will see us through, will make us better, and has our best interests at heart. I am grateful to see a book that will inspire us and lead us to make lasting, positive change for us and others whom we serve.

Hollis Milton
Superintendent of West Feliciana Parish Schools

I want to first dedicate this book to God the Father, Jesus Christ, my Lord and Savior, and the Holy Spirit, my comforter.

Secondly, to my wife, whom I was blessed with for thirty-eight years of marriage together. Love you always.

Thirdly, to my children and grandchildren, who have supported me throughout this journey.

Lastly, to my church family. I love you dearly.

CONTENTS

Unexpected Moment 3
The Grieving Process 9
Coping with the Unexpected 23
Trusting God When You Don't Understand 33
The Power of Memorial 45
Faith for the Journey 55
Bitter or Better? 67
You Can Do This 77
A Tribute to My Wife 81
Notes 91
About the Author 93
About Renown Publishing 97

INTRODUCTION

Unexpected Moment

March 26, 2020. A day that was seemingly uneventful, turned into a day I will never forget. I never envisioned that this date would hold such significance in my life. At the time, I didn't know I was experiencing my final days with my wife.

On March 26, my wife was in the midst of being quarantined in her bedroom at our home, based on the recommendation of her doctor. This was extremely difficult, because my wife was a "people person." The fact she couldn't be around her family was a tremendous challenge. So, on that night, my son, my daughter, and I sat right at the door of my and my wife's bedroom. We opened the door, sat in the hallway, and talked with her. This was our way of spending quality time with her.

At a certain point, my wife asked my daughter to sing a popular song entitled "Oceans."[1] This was one of her favorite worship songs. As my daughter sang, we all began to worship. It was a wonderful experience. After that, we spent the remainder of the evening hanging out and talking with her. In the midst of us enjoying our time together, she told me she was having shortness of breath more frequently. So, I called our doctor. He told her to go to the hospital in the morning to have an X-ray on her lungs, and he called in a prescription for her.

The X-ray that she was set to receive was one of several tests she received within that same week. Just a few days prior, March 23, 2020, she had received a flu and COVID-19 test. All of this transpired during the early part of the worldwide COVID-19 pandemic. Both tests were administered while she was in the vehicle. The flu test was first, and the results came back negative. Then she was tested for COVID-19, but we never received those results.

When we woke up the morning of March 27, 2020, to get ready, it took her a while to get dressed. We left the house that day with every intention of returning home. We picked up her medicine and then proceeded to the hospital. When we arrived, she received the X-ray, and her doctor decided to have her admitted into the emergency room to be evaluated by the doctor on duty. All I could do was sit in the emergency waiting room. After the doctor examined her, he came out and told me that her oxygen level was low and that they were going to have to rush her to a larger hospital where she could receive better care.

While I was waiting, my daughter called to get an update. At the time, I didn't want to answer the phone, because I didn't want to alarm anyone. However, I am glad I did since that would prove to be our last chance to see her. I told my daughter what was going on. She and my youngest son jumped in the car and drove to meet me at the initial hospital prior to her being transferred. They called my two oldest sons to tell them what was going on. They were not in close proximity, so they didn't have enough time to make it to the initial hospital. Instead, they decided they would meet us at the hospital she was being transferred to.

When the hospital personnel brought her out to put her into the ambulance, the three of us—my son, my daughter, and I—waved to her, and she gave us a thumbs up. We jumped into our cars and followed them to the next hospital; my two oldest sons met us there. When we got there, I tried to go into the emergency waiting room, like I'd done at the other hospital. However, they stopped me at the door and told me I couldn't go in. I was in shock. So, I asked them to give her phone to her, and they complied with my request. This was our only way of communicating with her initially; we all texted back and forth with her. Since no one was allowed to stay at the hospital with her, we told her we would stay at our church in Baton Rouge so that we would be as close as possible to her.

After that, everything started happening so quickly. That same day, March 27, I received a call at 11:00 p.m. It was my wife on the phone, with a doctor in the room. He told me he needed to sedate her and put her on the ventilator if she had any chance of surviving. He wanted permission to do so, because she didn't want to make that decision on her own.

I had one of my children call our doctor from their phone, because I didn't know what to do. I told him what the doctor at the hospital was saying, and our doctor said that if they thought putting her on the ventilator was the best option, then do it. So, my wife and I expressed our final words to each other. I told her that I loved her, and she said, "I love you, too." These were my final words to my wife. When we hung up, I began to weep, because everything was happening so fast. I had just spent the entire morning with her, and now, within the same day, I could no longer talk to her.

Then something rose up in me to fight for my wife. I started a prayer chain, with around-the-clock prayer for her healing, and people joined in from everywhere. The following eleven days were filled with pain and discomfort. My youngest son describes it as the "fastest yet slowest days of our lives." We literally sat around the phone waiting on a call from the hospital three times a day: Once in the morning. Once at noon. Once at night. This caused extreme anxiety for us. One minute it seemed like she was getting better. Then, it would get worse.

Because we couldn't be by her bedside, my children and I met at the hospital in the morning every day and prayed for her and everyone in that hospital. My sons' wives even met up with us when they could, to pray with us. Every time a doctor or nurse called me with an update, I offered them prayer, and they always accepted. I prayed with them over the phone that God would protect them and their families through this process.

I remember one nurse in particular, who spent eight of the eleven days with my wife. One day I asked her to put the phone to my wife's ear, even though I knew she was sedated. I was just hoping she could hear my voice. Out of the kindness of her heart, that nurse held her phone to my wife's ear for me. I told my wife again how much I loved her, and how I was looking forward to her returning back home.

On the morning of the day she transitioned home to be with the Lord—April 6, 2020—our family was on the hospital grounds praising God through song and praying. It was different that morning because we all felt an overwhelming peace come over us. We left there excited because of the peace we were experiencing. We were looking forward to her coming home.

After leaving the hospital, my daughter and I drove to our church in St. Francisville to take care of some business. As I drove up on the parking lot, the call came letting us know that my wife had gone home to the Lord. We were in shock, especially due to the way we had felt while we were at the hospital that morning. We were truly on an unexpected journey.

My wife was an amazing woman. She devoted her life to ministry, serving alongside me for thirty-eight years. This book is a tribute to her, and I hope it can be an encouragement to you as you walk through your own unexpected journeys.

CHAPTER ONE

The Grieving Process

Grief is not simply a moment in time. It is a collection of moments: some comforting and others uncomfortable, some heartwarming and others heartbreaking. It's a journey, with twists and turns along the way. And maybe most accurately, it's a *process*. As with any journey or process, there are choices to make along the way. To turn left or right? To stop or keep going? To travel quickly or meander through it?

My desire is that you will develop a close relationship with the Lord. However, if you are finding it difficult to believe in Him at this time, please open your heart to what I share about my personal journey. Regardless of where you are in terms of faith, you can reap the benefits of the wisdom contained in this book to help you navigate your grieving process.

I am sharing my grief experience and journey because I know that countless others are going through the same thing right now. In that single circumstance, we are connected. We are meant to support each other through this process, and I have been called to minister not only to myself, but also to you. Pastor T. D. Jakes offers encouragement to ministers with regard to "leading while bleeding."[2]

You will get through this. I am sure of it because we will be traveling together, along this crooked path, with an army of support: you, me, our supporters—and the undying love, direction, and encouragement of the Lord.

No One Should Grieve Alone

Grief is a serious condition. It has been described as a *deep* sorrow, especially that which is caused by someone's death.[3] This is no walk in the park. Grief is the worst of all sorrows.

So, how can we get through it? The key word in that question is *we*.

No one can, or should, grieve alone. You will need the help of others. If you choose to isolate yourself, you cannot take full advantage of the goodness that God has placed in your life—in the form of family, friends, your pastor, and even kind strangers.

Of course, as you grieve, there will be times when you're more comfortable being alone. You may need to have a good, hard cry. Or you may need to express anger. You may even need the quiet of an empty house to ask God, *"Why?"* This is to be expected during the stages of grief. However, if you allow these moments to extend into your everyday life, you simply cannot be victorious over grief.

We need God in order to navigate the wilds of the

grieving process. We also need other people—a strong, supportive base to listen to you, to hold your hand, to lift you up, and to share in your memories. Without this, depression (and all the dark roads it leads to) is imminent.

I know the value of a strong support base, because I've been blessed with one. First and foremost, the Lord, from whom I draw my strength to face each new day. I know that it can be tempting to turn away from the Lord in times of trouble, but in order to activate and move through this grieving process, you must turn toward Him.

During the first few days following my wife's death, it was hard for me to pray. What would I say? What would I ask for? How could I express the feelings I was having—feelings that even I wasn't sure how to define or manage?

So, for the first few days, I just sat quietly in the presence of the Lord to see what He would say to me. There were times when I would break down in His presence. I was just too emotional to pray. However, during that time, the Lord began to comfort and strengthen me so that He could speak to me on what steps I needed to take in this process.

If you haven't yet prayed during your grieving process, know that any thoughts you open to God will not be judged; they need not be edited. You simply need to open yourself up to Him and express your deep, innermost feelings.

There is no greater source of comfort than God. He is *love*, and therefore He is *comfort*. The apostle Paul wrote, "Blessed by God, even the Father of our Lord Jesus Christ, the Father of mercies, and the God of all comfort" (2 Corinthians 1:3). In other words, God can console us in every situation, circumstance, trial, or tribulation we may go through.

Verse 4 says, "Who comforteth us in all our tribulation; that we may be able to comfort them which are in any trouble, by the comfort wherewith we ourselves are comforted of God" (2 Corinthians 1:4). And there it is! A word from God that He will also work through those people who surround us. He will bring people into our lives who will walk alongside us through the grief process.

And here we have evidence that even if your relationship with God is not as open, honest, or active as it could be, you can open your heart and allow the Spirit to move in you, and you can also look to those who have the Spirit in them to help you along the way. Remember that God is everywhere. Even if you're not ready to pray, like I wasn't in those first days following my wife's death, know that others are there to bridge the gap, while God works through them.

It's also important to understand that God wants to be part of this grieving process. You are His child. He loves you with more love than the human mind can comprehend. He loves you so much that He gave His only Son to ensure that you could spend eternity with Him.

So as you grieve, if you have thoughts that God doesn't want to hear from you, or that God has bigger fish to fry, remember the love He has for you. As Paul wrote, "Be careful for nothing; but in everything by prayer and supplication with thanksgiving let your requests be made known unto God" (Philippians 4:6).

What Paul was really saying is that we should take *everything* to the Lord in prayer. God wants you to pour your heart out to Him. He doesn't mind you expressing just how you feel, what you're going through, the confusion you're feeling, the emotions you're not proud of. He wants to be your release. He wants you to come to Him, like a loving father wants his child to cry on his shoulder. He wants you to feel better after spending time with Him. He wants to pour strength and peace into you, because He has unlimited supplies of both.

Verse 7 goes on to say, "And the peace of God, which passeth all understanding, shall keep your hearts and minds through Christ Jesus" (Philippians 4:7). God will give you peace; there is no question. The only variable lies in whether or not you choose to accept that peace. Believe me, I've had moments when I wanted to quit. It would have been easier to think it couldn't get better—easier to reject God's offering of peace and comfort. But those moments were temporary. God stepped in, and I acknowledged His presence. In one particular instance, I opened my eyes in the morning to no other thought than my wife's passing. It hit me like a bucket of cold water in the face. But that wasn't all that was there. In the midst of that shock was God's peace. All I had to do was choose to receive it. And in that truth, I found the support I needed in that moment.

In order for that to happen, you must spend time in the presence of the Lord. Paul said it best when he told the church at Corinth that there will be others ready and able to comfort you, simply because they have received comfort from God and from their own support system (2 Corinthians 1:4). In this manner, God works through people to deliver what you need. He has a way of surrounding us with, or introducing us to, people who have gone through what we're experiencing. Just hearing someone say, "I understand," with some genuine understanding, can bring comfort.

God placed such people in my life. There are those who have come forward to share experiences similar to mine, from a different time in their lives. They have shared the emotions they felt and showed me there are people who can completely relate to what I'm going through.

My siblings have stood alongside me, their brother. They have called and offered encouragement. My children have stood with their father—we communicate every day. My pastor friends, both local and from across the country, have also reached out. My church family has supported me as well, and I can't thank them enough for everything they've done for me and my children. My wife's family members have called, and they've reached out to my children through social media. And I can't forget my friends: they have called, talked, shared, and encouraged. They have sent tokens of love, like cards and flowers.

I have been blessed with a remarkable support system. And you can have that, too. A lot of times, when we're in pain, we tend to shut ourselves off from those who want to lend a hand. They may not be the people we expect, but God will always send help—even if it's just one person. It might be a family member or a friend, but it can also be a stranger. We simply need to open ourselves to all the possibilities, and accept love, support, and help when it comes.

Isolating yourself rejects this gift from God. Trust me

when I tell you that He will send the help you need, even in your darkest hour. If you are receptive to that, you won't miss it.

He's letting us know that even when we feel all alone in the world, we're not.

Allow those people to come and walk alongside you. Allow them to lend a hand of support, to help you get through this process. You need them; you will not get through this alone.

Imagination Can Be the Enemy

We often think of our imagination as a helper, but in times like this, it can go to places that trigger emotions that aren't necessary, or that will lead us down dangerous roads. Things can hit your mind and induce anger, frustration, sorrow, depression, and so much more. Your imagination is the faculty that forms new ideas, images, concepts, or external objects that are not present to the senses. Put simply, what your imagination sees *isn't real*.

The enemy will infiltrate your imagination, trying to convince you to throw in the towel and say it's not worth going on. But you have to take control of your thoughts. You have a choice.

You can replay scenes that you're not proud of, or wonder what you could have done differently, or blame yourself or others. But then you have to decide: will you dwell there or move on to find happier thoughts?

Paul had the answer: "Finally, brethren, whatsoever things are true, whatsoever things are honest, whatsoever things are just, whatsoever things are pure, whatsoever things are lovely, whatsoever things are of good report; if there be any virtue, and if there be any praise, think on these things" (Philippians 4:8).

Just as you should never isolate yourself during grief, you should never allow your thoughts to wander down a negative road. Yes, you can have negative emotions. Acknowledge them, feel them, and then move forward.

If you choose a negative thought pattern, the implications will be serious: "For the weapons of our warfare are not carnal, but mighty through God to the pulling down of strongholds. Casting down imaginations, and every high thing that exalteth itself against the knowledge of God, and bringing into captivity every thought to the obedience of Christ" (2 Corinthians 10:4–5).

That phrase "casting down" means to strike it down, just like a spiked ball in a volleyball game. Get the negativity out of your mind as quickly as possible. Strongholds can show up at this time in your life and you won't be able to break free. I have watched people fail to break free of strongholds that have formed in their lives right after the loss of a loved one. It did not end well.

If you commit to checking these negative thoughts before they take over, you can open yourself to happy thoughts that God presents you with. At the most unexpected times, I find myself thinking about the thirty-eight years my wife and I spent together. Her smile and her laugh. Our loving marriage, enjoying each other. The legacy she left behind in her children. I still tear up, but I don't park myself in the negative thoughts, which can turn into strongholds. If you supply them with even the smallest bit of power, they will control your life. Bitterness, resentment, and depression (which can lead to suicide) are just a few examples.

Today is the day. Do not even attempt to walk through this alone. The Lord is waiting to accompany you. He's waiting to fill your mind with happy thoughts, and to connect you to people who will act as channels from Him, to supply the strength and peace you'll need to be victorious over grief.

Acceptance: Why Is It So Difficult?

And when all the congregation saw that Aaron was dead, they mourned for Aaron thirty days, even all the house of Israel.
—Numbers 20:29

As you move through the grieving process, it's important to understand that you don't have to be all right with this; you don't have to be okay with everything that's happened. In fact, you don't *ever* have to be.

I know you're not all right with it—because I'm not, either. But acceptance is different. You must accept the reality that your loved one is physically gone and recognize it as a permanent reality. If you're having difficulty with acceptance, know that you're not alone. I have days when I struggle with it, too.

Why is the death of a loved one so hard to accept? My children and I, as well as my wife's family, have discussed this question. And for us, we have found that three things, in particular, are trying to stand in the way of our acceptance:

1. We feel like we've just woken up from a bad dream. We all share the same notion: it hasn't yet settled in, and we find it hard to believe she's no longer with us.

2. Life is different now, that's for sure. But we are struggling with knowing that it will never be like it used to be.

3. It's hard to envision a future without her. We don't even want to think about it. My wife and I talked about the future—about the things we wanted to accomplish, the fun we wanted to have, and the things we wanted to see happen. We were planning our future together, and now that future doesn't have half of the equation in it.

I know you're feeling these same things. I have spoken with a number of people who have lost a loved one, and they have had these thoughts and feelings as well.

But when you reach the point of acceptance—when you know that God still has a plan for your life going forward, even though it will be different than you'd expected—then you can move forward with peace and joy.

Help with Acceptance

And the children of Israel wept for Moses in the plains of Moab thirty days: so the days of weeping and mourning for Moses were ended.
—*Deuteronomy 34:8*

Grief doesn't last a specific period of time for every person. The process is different for all of us. But one thing is for sure: when we reach true acceptance, then we can begin to move forward in life.

In the midst of mourning and grieving, we have a promise of God's comfort, and He knows exactly what we need in each moment. But how can you welcome that? What can you do to deal with this challenge?

1. Know who holds the future. It is God, and God alone. Your future is in His hands, and you are not stepping into this alone. You will not have a clear picture of what lies ahead; however, remember that God says, "For I know the thoughts that I think toward you, saith the LORD, thoughts of peace, and not of evil, to give you an expected end" (Jeremiah 29:11). God the Father is still in control. Jesus is still Lord. Life is worth living because He lives. "The steps of a good man are ordered by the LORD: and he delightith in his way" (Psalm 37:23). That's why you still have to seek Him; He holds your future, and He knows how to give it to you step by step. He will order your moves so you can step into what He has in store for you.

2. Know that God is able to keep you. "Thou shalt keep them, O LORD, thou shalt preserve them from this generation for ever" (Psalm 12:7). He will preserve you, keep you, and sustain you. "For the LORD shall be thy confidence, and shall keep thy foot from being taken" (Proverbs 3:26). The word *keep* means "to cause to continue in a specified condition, position, course, etc."[4] God will make sure you stay on course, as long as you commit to moving forward in what He has ordained and established for your life. The Lord is in touch with your feelings; He knows you. You need only go to Him.

Your move toward acceptance may be slow, and you may have difficulty seeing light on the other side at this moment. Just know that "the LORD will give strength unto His people; the LORD will bless His people with peace" (Psalm 29:11). You don't have to find the strength or the peace within yourself. God will supply that.

Keep Moving Forward

Moving through the grieving process and coming out the other side with God is not set to happen in any specific timeframe. Where you are is where you will move on from, and it will happen in time.

You must remove guilt from your thought life. Do not feel guilty about where you're at in the grieving process—remember, it's a developing journey, and it takes time. You also have to let go of the idea that you're betraying your loved one by moving on and enjoying your life. God's plan for you does not stop when He brings your loved ones home.

There will be bumps and rough patches along the way;

I still have my moments. But I know that God will preserve me and show me His plan going forward. He offers me comfort at every stage, and I am assured of that when He tells us, "Blessed are they that mourn; for they shall be comforted" (Matthew 5:4).

As you strive for acceptance, pray the serenity prayer: "God grant me the serenity to accept the things I cannot change, the courage to change the things I can, and the wisdom to know the difference." This sums up God's will for us in just one sentence.

Even though so many things feel uncertain at this time, I am confident that you and I will get through this together, with the help of the Lord.

WORKBOOK

Chapter One Reflection

Prompt: Take some time to simply *be* with God while you experience all of your thoughts and feelings in the midst of your grief. Don't worry about praying intelligible thoughts, making requests, or even giving thanks. Just be with God. Let Him hold you through it. In a notebook or journal, feel free to jot down anything that comes to your mind during this time. But don't feel pressured to come up with something; you don't have to write anything if you don't feel like it. Just know that is an option if it supports you in the moment.

CHAPTER TWO

Coping with the Unexpected

And, behold, there came a great wind from the wilderness, and smote the four corners of the house, and it fell upon the young men, and they are dead; and I only am escaped alone to tell thee.
—*Job 1:19*

We often find ourselves at a loss for what to do when faced with the unexpected. We plan our days, our months, our years, and our lives—and at any time, one thing can happen that seems to turn it all on its head.

That's because we make plans without knowing God's plan for us. Sometimes, when the unexpected happens, we have to remember that the Lord knows the road ahead, and what we expect isn't always part of that journey.

Trust in the Midst of the Unexpected

Job had a sequence of unexpected events take place in his life, all in one day. By *unexpected* I mean unforeseen or startling—not just surprises, but things that have the potential to upend everything as we'd envisioned it.

We've all experienced this on different levels. Maybe you've had problems in a relationship, or you or a loved one has had health issues arise. Perhaps you've been faced with the aftermath of a sudden tragedy in your family or your community. Maybe one of your children delivered some unwelcome news, or you found out that you'd been betrayed by someone close to you. Or maybe, like me, someone you love went home to be with the Lord.

In times like these, it can be easy to start spiraling downward, questioning why such a thing would happen to you, or railing against God because you don't have answers to unanswerable questions.

But we don't have to be angry with God. He wants us to open up and express our feelings of frustration and confusion so He can minister to us with the comfort we so desperately need. Nowhere else on the face of the earth will you find the comfort God can give—and when you find it in other people, in a book, in a movie, in a phrase, or in a song—that, too, ultimately comes from God.

He knows you're discouraged. He knows you're having trouble understanding why this happened. And yet, His arms are open wide. You are His child, and He wants you to turn to Him.

The Scriptures are filled with people who did just that. They were instructed, "Trust in Him at all times; ye people, pour out your heart before Him: God is a refuge for us" (Psalm 62:8).

Why is it so important to go to God and find safety with Him? Because when we get caught up in asking "Why?"

and are stuck there, it causes us to tunnel deeper and deeper into a dark place, farther away from our Father. There is always a path back, but the farther you stray from His light, the more desolate your life on earth can seem—and that leads nowhere good.

Looking for an explanation when there is no earthly explanation will stop you from moving forward, and you will never reach your destination of peace and acceptance.

Job's Choice, and Ours

When these unexpected things happen—a death, the loss of a job, a financial setback, the loss of a friend, or any number of other misfortunes—we need to stop asking "Why?" and start quieting ourselves and preparing to listen for the still, small voice of the Lord. He will speak to you in your most difficult moments. Believe me, I know how challenging it can be to navigate through this. But He will help you. And just like we're told in Hebrews 4:14–16, we may obtain mercy and grace in our time of need.

In the Scriptures, Job lost his family, his possessions, his substance—everything he had. But he had a choice. In this midst of his pain and confusion, this was the response he chose: "Then Job arose, and rent his mantle, and shaved his head, and fell down upon the ground, and worshipped" (Job 1:20).

Job made the right choice, and it's a choice each of us has the option to make. He had not lost God, and he turned toward the Father in his time of most profound need. When he chose to do so, he learned that God was his everything.

Now, I'm not suggesting that the choice is a simple one to make. Your mind is fogged with grief. You aren't thinking clearly. And you may not feel like you have the energy to take on this type of mindset right now.

But when you make the choice to turn to God, He will supply you with the strength you're lacking. All of the reasons you might be hesitant to turn to Him will be resolved with the act of turning toward Him.

When we make the right choices, we feel stronger after steering our way through unexpected happenings. When we ask God to fortify us with His strength and peace, we come out the other side better for having known and trusted Him.

If that sounds like something you'd like to experience, then here are three things to do every time something unexpected happens:

1. Understand that what feels unexpected to you is not unexpected to Him. The Lord is an all-knowing God, and He will sustain you even if His plan is different from yours. Remember that He knew you before you were formed in your mother's womb (Jeremiah 1:5). He fashioned your destiny eons before you were born. Nothing in God's world is unexpected—or unnecessary.

> *Cast thy burden upon the LORD, and he shall sustain thee:*
> *He shall never suffer the righteous to be moved.*
> **—Psalm 55:22**

> *Yeah, forty years didst thou sustain them in the wilderness, so that they lacked nothing; their clothes not waxed old, and their feet swelled not.*
> **—Nehemiah 9:21**

> *Lord, how are they increased that trouble me! Many are they that rise up against me. Many there be which say of my soul, there is no help for him in God. But thou, O LORD, art a shield for me; my glory, and the lifter of mine head. I cried unto the LORD with my voice, and He heard me out of His holy hill. I laid me down and slept; I awaked; for the LORD sustained me.*
> **—Psalm 3:1–5**

2. Put your trust solely in Him. He already knows you need Him in this moment. Trust is a firm belief; it is being able to depend upon someone or something's ability and reliability.[5] You can count on God. You can trust Him. No one or nothing is more reliable, and He has shown us this with what He has accomplished.

> *Trust in the LORD with all thine heart; and lean not unto thine own understanding.*
> **—Proverbs 3:5**

> *Now thanks be unto God, which always causeth us to triumph in Christ, and maketh manifest the savour of His knowledge by us in every place.*
> **—2 Corinthians 2:14**

3. Know that He still has an awesome plan in store for

you. The future is no less bright because of this unexpected moment in time. This is a shift in your life—albeit a traumatic one in this instant—but please know that the Lord still has a great future in store for you.

> *For thus saith the LORD, That after seventy years be accomplished at Babylon I will visit you, and perform my good word toward you, in causing you to return to this place.*
>
> *For I know the thoughts that I think toward you, saith the LORD, thoughts of peace, and not of evil, to give you an expected end.*
> —*Jeremiah 29:10-11*

> *And the LORD turned the captivity of Job, when he prayed for his friends: also the LORD gave Job twice as much as he had before. Then came there unto him all his brethren, and all his sisters, and they that had been of his acquaintance before, and did eat bread with him in his house: and they bemoaned him, and comforted him over all the evil that the LORD had brought upon him: every man also gave him a piece of money, and every one an earring of gold. So the LORD blessed the latter end of Job more than his beginning: for he had fourteen thousand sheep, and six thousand camels, and a thousand yoke of oxen, and a thousand she asses.*
> —*Job 42:10-12*

It's human nature to panic, or worry, or get angry, or slip into a negative thought pattern when something happens that was not expected. But even in these moments of utter shock, it's crucial that we trust God to take us to a place of serenity, where we can work toward remaining calm, at peace, and without trouble in our hearts.

With God, you can maintain poise in difficult,

unforeseen circumstances. He wants this for you, as we are reminded in Philippians:

> *Be careful for nothing; but in everything by prayer and supplication with thanksgiving let your requests be made known unto God. And the peace of God, which passeth all understanding, shall keep your hearts and minds through Christ Jesus.*
> —**Philippians 4:6-7**

Grieving the Unexpected Loss of My Wife

When the unexpected happened to me, I found myself sitting in a place I never thought I'd be at this time in my life. I am grieving the loss of my wife, and grief sure is a hard place to exist.

I have struggled to find the words to describe how I feel, because this is the first time I've felt grief this profound. But here's the best way I know to illustrate it: I feel like Jesus in the garden of Gethsemane. The spiritual side of Him understood the victory on the other side of the price He was about to pay for our sins, but the human side was struggling with it to the point that His soul was exceedingly sorrowful. This is significant to me, because the soul is the seat of our thoughts, feelings, and will.

We know grief is deep sorrow, especially that which is caused by someone's death. That is what Jesus was feeling in the garden as He prepared for His own death. He was divine but felt all the things you and I feel, because He was human as well.

This is how I choose to describe my own grief, because

the spiritual part of me knows that my wife is in a better place and I rejoice in that knowledge. The apostle Paul described it like this in Philippians 1:23: "For I am a strait betwixt two, having a desire to depart, and to be with Christ; which is far better." And yet, the human part of me is struggling to navigate the process of grief. I know I will see her again, and our reunion will be one filled with incredible joy. But I'm having trouble letting go of all the plans we were making, and looking forward to, on this side of life.

My human mind cannot understand why it had to happen this way. But I also know that my human mind is not capable of comprehending the magnitude of God's plan. I can't claim to know the reason she died like she did, and I can't explain why it had to happen now. Sometimes I feel like I just don't know where to turn. What do you do when God says *no*?

I know the Lord could have healed my wife. He has the power to do anything. I do not know why He didn't, but I am not bitter toward Him. Everything I am and everything I have become is because of Him. I shared thirty-eight beautiful years with my wife because of Him.

In the midst of this unexpected event, I have found God's comfort in countless places and in many people. I am not the only one who's been affected by my wife's passing. My church has also lost its first lady. My children have lost their mother. Her family has lost their daughter, sister, niece, and cousin, and there are countless other lives she has touched. We are navigating this together, with the support of the Lord and one another.

You, too, have the peace and comfort of the Lord at

your disposal. Even when the unexpected happens, you can rest in knowing that the people you need will come to your aid and God will be there, just waiting to hear you. This is His promise, and there is nothing more trustworthy in heaven or on earth.

WORKBOOK

Chapter Two Reflection

Prompt: In a journal or notebook, write out a prayer expressing your trust in God even in your difficult circumstance. And if you are struggling to find the trust—struggling to turn to Him—then ask Him for the strength to do so.

CHAPTER THREE

Trusting God When You Don't Understand

Trust in the LORD with all thine heart; and lean not unto thine own understanding.
—***Proverbs 3:5***

The writer Solomon spoke these words of wisdom to us. He assured us that we cannot possibly understand all that the Lord is doing. God's plan—His end goal—is beyond our comprehension, and attempting to understand His reasoning would be futile.

Instead, we are called to trust in the Lord without fail. We are encouraged to open our hearts and minds to His Word so we may receive His grace, which will guide us toward the fulfillment of His plan.

This can be simpler in times when life seems easy. When everything is going smoothly, we have no trouble trusting in God's wisdom and justice. It feels like our plan is His plan. It all makes sense.

But then, when something unexpected happens—something we don't feel like we deserve, or something that doesn't fit our expectations—it's easy to question God's plan for us. Is He teaching us a lesson? Testing us? Punishing us? Telling us we're on the wrong path?

The fact that these questions only come up when we don't see the sense in something that's happened proves His plan is always bigger than ours. Remember what He said in Isaiah 55:9: "For as the heavens are higher than the earth, so are my ways higher than your ways, and my thoughts than your thoughts."

So, how do we maintain trust in God when it feels like our lives have been turned upside down?

The answer is faith.

Lean Not on Your Own Understanding

American author, filmmaker, and photographer Jon Raymond said, "You can't know what you don't know."[6] And when it comes to God, it's important to understand that what you don't know—what you can't know—He does.

That's why you must trust Him. When you don't understand why something happened, you cannot lean on your own understanding—because it's not adequate.

In my own time of trouble, I have defaulted to God. I cannot grasp the reason for my wife having to leave this world. But He knows. God has His reasons, and they are bigger and better than I can imagine.

And so, I choose to have faith. I choose to place full confidence in the wisdom and knowledge of God. You, too, can rest in this place of faith, confidence, and trust in the Lord.

Here are four truths that have helped me to trust, even in the worst of times. I believe they will help you as well.

1. God is all-knowing. That means there's nothing He doesn't know. He knows the past, the present, and the future. He sees and knows all things, even though we are limited in this way. That's why we must trust in Him when we don't understand. We don't see what He sees, and we don't know what He knows. When it seems likes He has changed the course of your life through an unexpected event, it hasn't really changed at all. The plan was always so, and it's playing out this way because He knows the end, which He designed.

> *Why, seeing times are not hidden from the Almighty, do they that know him not see his days?*
> —*Job 24:1*

> *For if our heart condemn us, God is greater than our heart, and knoweth all things.*
> —*1 John 3:20*

> *Remember the former things of old: for I am God, and there is none else; I am God, and there is none like Me, declaring the end from the beginning, and from ancient times the things that are not yet done, saying, My counsel shall stand, and I will do all my pleasure.*
> —*Isaiah 46:9–10*

> *For we know in part, and we prophesy in part.*
> —***1 Corinthians 13:9***

2. God does not operate in the same human ways that we do. He doesn't think, reason, or see the way we do, either.

> *For My thoughts are not your thoughts, neither are your ways My ways, sayeth the Lord. For as the heavens are higher than the earth, so are My ways higher than your ways, and My thoughts than your thoughts.*
> —***Isaiah 55:8–9***

Our perceptions always color our beliefs and what we see as reality. If you're anything like me, you can look back on your life and think of things you could have done differently. This is proof that our "knowing" at any given moment is not as vast as our Father's.

> *O the depth of the riches both of the wisdom and knowledge of God! How unsearchable are His judgments, and His ways past finding out! For who hath known the mind of the Lord? Or who hath been His counsellor?*
> —***Romans 11:33–34***

In order to trust in God, we must recognize that we do not (and cannot) know everything about Him. His timing is not always the same as ours, and this is to serve His greater plan. Psalm 18:30 says, "As for God, His way is perfect: the word of the Lord is tried: He is a buckler to all those that trust in Him." And we must accept that we can trust His plan because His way is the best way.

3. Above all, God is good, and has been very kind and generous to us. Even when life surprises us with unexpected sorrow or pain, we must trust that the greater plan is for our benefit. Trusting Him begins with accepting this as truth.

> *The LORD is good to all: and His tender mercies are over all His works.*
> **—Psalm 145:9**

> *Truly God is good to Israel, even to such as are of a clean heart.*
> **—Psalm 73:1**

> *And we know that all things work together for good to them that love God, to them who are called according to His purpose.*
> **—Romans 8:28**

4. Know that God is love. There is no evil in Him at all. He loves you. Just let that sink in for a moment. Because He loves you unconditionally, He will always have your best interests at heart. His love is unending, and it will always protect and keep you.

> *Beloved, let us love one another: for love is of God; and*

> *every one that loveth is born of God, and knoweth God. He that loveth not knoweth not God; for God is love.*
> —*1 John 4:7–8*

> *Love worketh no ill to his neighbor: therefore love is the fulfilling of the law.*
> —*Romans 13:10*

> *Who shall separate us from the love of Christ? Shall tribulation, or distress, or persecution, or famine, or nakedness, or peril, or sword? As it is written, For thy sake we are killed all the day long; we are accounted as sheep for the slaughter. Nay, in all these things we are more than conquerors through him that loved us. For I am persuaded, that neither death, nor life, nor angels, nor principalities, nor powers, nor things present, nor things to come, nor height, nor depth, nor any other creature, shall be able to separate us from the love of God, which is in Christ Jesus our Lord.*
> —*Romans 8:35–39*

When something that's happened goes beyond our understanding, it can feel difficult to rely on God, whose voice might be drowned out by all the noise of what's happening here and now, on earth. Lean not on your own understanding, but rather on the truth that God's plan is beyond what you are capable of comprehending. Then, no matter what happens here, you shall be victorious.

The Benefits of Trusting in Him

Trust in God is so important—especially in troubled times. This can't be overstated and deserves to be delved into more deeply.

Proverbs 3:5 reminds us that trust goes beyond our human reasoning or ability to comprehend. This means that searching our minds to find evidence for trusting God is futile. The full will of God cannot be grasped by the human mind. The Bible tells us we can only know in part.

> *Remember the former things of old: for I am God, and there is none else; I am God, and there is none like me. ... Calling a ravenous bird from the east, the man that executeth my counsel from a far country; yea, I have spoken it, I will also bring it to pass; I have purposed it, I will also do it.*
> **—Isaiah 46:9, 11**

Remember that God is working all events after the plan and purpose of His own will.

We know that God is love, and so His will is love as well. We know that everything that happens is within God's knowledge and plan—of His *own* will. Therefore, all things that happen are products of God's unconditional love for us. And so, what reason do we have not to trust Him?

Being unable to comprehend what has happened is not a good reason, because we already know that God's ways and thoughts are unlike ours. This is not for us to comprehend. God does not want us to understand it; He just wants us to trust Him in the midst of it all. It doesn't matter how we think it should go. It's not a puzzle to solve or an answer to find.

Every day, we trust in things we can't explain but that we, humans, have made. Human hands have created airplanes, ships, space shuttles, submarines, bridges, cell phones, and computer programs—and we use, and trust in, all of them.

Advantages come along with that trust. We get to go places by air and sea, see new things, meet new people, make connections, see the beauty of God's creation, and much more. We trust in engineering and countless technologies, even though we couldn't build it or explain its operations for ourselves.

And yet, we doubt God's power. God, who is far greater than all these things.

So ,what are the advantages that come along with trusting God?

1. We are blessed. "Kiss the Son, lest he be angry, and ye perish from the way, when his wrath is kindled but a little. Blessed are all they that put their trust in him" (Psalm 2:12). The word *blessed* means to be "endowed with divine favor and protection."[7] It can also mean to be fortunate.[8] Who wouldn't want that? All that's required is to trust in the Lord. God will take control and make sure things go well.

2. He will defend us. "But let all those that put their trust in thee rejoice: let them ever shout for joy, because thou defendest them: let them also that love thy name be joyful in thee" (Psalm 5:11). Who doesn't want joy that's big enough to cause boisterous rejoicing? Rejoice in the fact that God is willing to defend you. He will fight for you and speak up for you if you trust in Him.

3. We are helped. "The LORD is my strength and my shield; my heart trusted in him, and I am helped: therefore my heart greatly rejoiceth; and with my song will I praise him" (Psalm 28:7). We all need the Lord's help. I need it right now, and so do you. You have a lot to handle, and accepting help will make it easier. So, why not trust in the greatest Helper you will ever know? Why not take His hand and accept the assistance of God, who wants nothing more than to aid you with His infinite wisdom and love? These are unmatched advantages to trusting the Lord, without a doubt.

4. We receive God's goodness. "Oh how great is thy goodness, which thou hast laid up for them that fear thee; which thou hast wrought for them that trust in thee before the sons of men!" (Psalm 31:19). God's goodness is overflowing, and He's just waiting to pour it over you. He has many kind acts to bestow on you, but in order to receive all those benefits, you must trust in Him.

5. God directs our paths. "Trust in the LORD with all thine heart; and lean no unto thine own understanding. In all thy ways acknowledge Him, and he shall direct thy paths" (Proverbs 3:5–6). For, "the steps of a good man are ordered by the LORD: and He delightith in his way" (Psalm 37:23). When we trust God, He will make the path He intended for us clear. He will offer direction and guidance to those who have faith in Him.

6. We are filled with peace. "Thou wilt keep him in perfect peace, whose mind is stayed on thee: because he trusteth in thee" (Isaiah 26:3). When you place your trust in the Lord without reservation, you will experience a sense of inner calm, rest, and tranquility. And from this place, you will move toward accepting whatever is happening (or has happened) in your life. You will see it as part of God's plan, and you will be able to let go of trying to explain it or needing to understand it. You can simply live joyfully—in God's presence and under His protection.

There are a number of tremendous benefits that come with fully trusting God. And every one of them—from being blessed, to gaining help, to experiencing joy—is something we pursue throughout our lives, in good times and in bad. God is extending this to each of us. All He asks is that we move forward with Him in confidence, having faith that His Word is true and trusting in His all-knowing power and providence.

What He's asking of us is so simple, so little, compared to what He gave for us. Calling what we get in return "benefits" hardly does justice to all the gifts He's ready to give. Especially now, while you are hurting. You are His child. Go to Him.

WORKBOOK

Chapter Three Reflection

Prompt: In a journal or notebook write the ways—big and small—you have experienced God's faithfulness and goodness, particularly in times of pain, confusion, and grief.

CHAPTER FOUR

The Power of Memorial

As you move forward along your journey of grief, you will see that healing happens when you can focus on the happy memories you and your loved one shared together during their time on the earth. Take the time to focus on the unforgettable moments that you shared. And in this, you can find gratitude and appreciation for the gift you were given.

Those memories cannot be taken from you. Your life as a whole has been enriched because of that person you were blessed enough to have loved. This is reason to rejoice. It's also the reason memorials bring so much comfort to those who are grieving. That's why I suggest you set something up to memorialize the one you've lost.

The Meaning of a Memorial

On Mother's Day and every day, I will forever honor my wife as the mother of my children. I will also honor her as the mother of my Faith, Hope, and Love church family.

That's in my own heart and mind. I will hold it there to bring me comfort in good times and in bad. But there's more. A physical memorial to commemorate my wife's life will act as a tangible portrayal of her life—one that was a demonstration of Christ's love here on earth.

Memorials have power. Not just the power to remind us of those we have loved, but the power to keep their values, talents, passions, and methods—their gifts from God that they expressed on earth—alive and well.

Memorials jog our memories. They bring back the joy we experienced while being with our loved one and remind us to continue spreading the goodness they planted here.

The word *memorial* means something that is designed to preserve the memory of a person or event. We all know that memories fade. We might remember events and people, but as time passes, the sights and sounds begin to dull, the colors become less vivid, and we might start to question the order of events—but if you have a memorial that solidifies those things in your mind, you're less likely to forget.

When we talk about preserving something, we maintain that thing in its original or existing state. A memorial preserves our memories by stamping them in time and in our minds.

This is not only a human principle. God the Father spoke about this throughout Scripture. Here are a couple examples:

> *And it came to pass, when all the people were clean passed*

over Jordan, that the LORD spoke unto Joshua, saying, Take you twelve men out of the people, out of every tribe a man, and command ye them, saying, Take you hence out of the midst of Jordan, out of the place where the priests' feet stood firm, twelve stones, and ye shall carry them over with you, and leave them in the lodging place, where ye shall lodge this night. Then Joshua called the twelve men, whom he had prepared of the children of Israel, out of every tribe a man: And Joshua said unto them, pass over before the ark of the LORD your God into the midst of Jordan, and take you up every man of you a stone upon his shoulder, according unto the number of the tribes of the children of Israel: That this may be a sign among you, that when your children ask their fathers in time to come, saying, What mean ye by these stones? Then ye shall answer them, That the waters of Jordan were cut off before the ark of the covenant of the LORD; when it passed over Jordan, the waters of Jordan were cut off: and these stones shall be for a memorial unto the children of Israel forever.

—Joshua 4:1–7

There came unto him a woman having an alabaster box of very precious ointment, and poured it on his head, as he sat at meat. But when his disciples saw it, they had indignation, saying, To what purpose is this waste? For this ointment might have been sold for much, and given to the poor. When Jesus understood it, he said unto them, Why trouble ye the woman? for she hath wrought a good work upon me. For ye have the poor always with you; but me ye have not always. For in that she hath poured this ointment on my body, she did it for my burial. Verily I say unto you, Wheresoever this gospel shall be preached in the whole world, there shall also this, that this woman hath done, be told for a memorial of her.

—Matthew 26:7–13

God understands our grief. He also understands the

power of physical memorials to keep us connected to our loved ones. But why is this so important to Him? Why does He want this for us?

The Importance of Memorials

As I alluded to earlier, memorials allow the essence of a person who has died to live on, here with us, so that we can remember what they've taught us, shown us, and helped us to see.

Our loved one does not have to have be physically with us in order to live on through us. Friends might cite a physical resemblance, or say things like, "You remind me of her." They might add, "That's something she would say!" These things are evidence that you were connected, but there's more. You can communicate their goodness through the work you do, the fun you have, the service you give, the love you show, and the relationships you nurture.

When we keep their memories alive, then who they were on earth is alive as well. The goodness they enacted goes on. The smiles they caused continue. The love they expressed is multiplied.

And memorials initiate all those good things. Loved ones will not be forgotten by those they influenced, and their memory will travel through generations to come—as long as that memorial is in place.

And the LORD spake unto Moses, saying, Sanctify unto me all the firstborn, whatsoever openeth the womb among the

children of Israel, both of man and of beast: it is mine. And Moses said unto the people, Remember this day, in which ye came out from Egypt, out of the house of bondage; for by strength of hand the LORD brought you out from this place: there shall no leavened bread be eaten. This day came ye out in the month Abib. And it shall be when the LORD shall bring thee into the land of the Canaanites, and the Hittites, and the Amorites, and the Hivites, and the Jebusites, which he swear unto thy fathers to give thee, a land flowing with milk and honey, that thou shalt keep this service in this month. Seven days thou shalt eat unleavened bread, and in the seventh day shall be a feast to the LORD. Unleavened bread shall be eaten seven days; and there shall no leavened bread be seen with thee, neither shall there be leaven seen with thee in all thy quarters. And thou shalt shew thy son in that day, saying, This is done because of that which the LORD did unto me when I came forth out of Egypt. And it shall be for a sign unto thee upon thine hand, and for a memorial between thine eyes, that the LORD's law may be in thy mouth: for with a strong hand hath the LORD brought thee out of Egypt.
—*Exodus 13:1-9*

What qualifies as a "sign unto thee?" Anything that you feel in your heart best represents your deceased loved one. It can be a gravestone, a video montage, a photo, a painting, a scholarship fund, a brick in a wall, a book about their life, a piece of jewelry—anything. The choice is yours alone.

A Memorial for My Wife

My family and I are working on a memorial for my wife as I write this. We want her to be known by all of her grandchildren, great-grandchildren, and great-great-grandchildren. In other words, we are finding comfort in creating something that will ensure she will not be forgotten.

Again, this is the power of a memorial. Not only does it keep all of the goodness associated with her alive, but it also offers the comfort of knowing we will never lose her memory. Her legend will live, as she does in heaven.

As my family and I work on my wife's memorial, we are discovering the life He has in store for us going forward. I think you'll discover the same when you start to think about how you will memorialize your loved one.

We Found the Life He Had for Us

When I think back on my wife's life and the life we shared together, I can't help but think of Jesus' resurrection and the promise of new life with Him: "Know ye not, that so many of us as were baptized into Jesus Christ were baptized into his death? Therefore we are buried with him by baptism into death: that like as Christ was raised up from the dead by the glory of the Father, even so we also should walk in newness of life" (Romans 6:3–4).

Matthew tells us how this has been made possible: "Then said Jesus unto his disciples, 'If any man will come after me, let him deny himself, and take up his cross, and follow me. For whosoever will save his life shall lose it: and whosoever will lose his life for my sake shall find it'" (Matthew 16:24–25).

At the ages of nineteen and seventeen years old, respectively, my wife and I walked away from the lives we had been living and found the new, remarkable life God had waiting for us. That life was one we would live together, in Him. And for thirty-eight years, we lived in Him.

Do I miss my wife? Of course I do. Does it hurt? Absolutely. Do I wish I could share more years with her? Without a doubt.

In the midst of all of this, I must give thanks to the Lord for blessing me with her for the time we had. Some people never get to enjoy having a lifelong partner. And so, her memorial will also be a tribute to that.

A Memorial to Share with God

If it weren't for God's action in our lives, Robbin and I would not have found each other. We would not have known we were right for each other at such young ages.

Of course, we had our share of trials and tribulations along the way, but He also placed many generous victories on the path we walked together. My wife and I never had to doubt that God was at the center of our marriage. He made that known in numerous ways, every day.

At the age of eighteen, Robbin started working with teenage girls and founded Young Women for Christ. When we were twenty-one and twenty-three years of age, we built our first house together. A year later, we started our own business, which tripled in three short years, prompting me to leave the post office and work for our company full-time.

Our marriage bore the weight of all this, but the Lord healed it as needed. Through that healing, we recognized we had been charged with helping to repair others' marriages, too. And so, we started pastoring at the ages of twenty-five-and twenty-seven-years old. My first book was authored with the help of my wife.

During this whirlwind, we were blessed with five beautiful children—one of whom is with my wife in heaven now. We bought our second home, co-authored a book called *A Love Like This*, hosted our own telecast for a total of twelve years, and then opened a second location for Faith, Hope, and Love Worship Center.

Next, we built our third house, where I currently reside, and started hosting marriage retreats in a number of states. There was our school initiative, where Robbin founded G.E.M.S., the Our Flip programs, and Little G.E.M.S., and where I founded West Fellas. There were more than a thousand girls in her program, and we were awarded the Apple award for our work in schools.

We traveled to so many places together, stayed in some of the finest hotels, ate gourmet food in upscale restaurants, and attended major events, and she shopped everywhere we went. We had an amazing life together, but most of all, we simply enjoyed each other. We worked together, prayed together, and played together. Just being together was enough for us. My sister said it best: "You two operate as one flesh." And she was right: we did just about everything *together*.

This life we built—this life we lived together—was found together in Christ. We owe it all to Him. She was a remarkable woman, and I will forever be grateful to God for bringing us together. During her last year on earth, she said these words to me: "The Lord has given me everything I have dreamed of." She felt fulfilled in her life, and I can rest well knowing that she expressed that before she died.

Isn't that all any of us can ask for? To know that we have followed Christ's directives for the life we were meant to live? And that we have been given everything we ever needed?

What a life! What a gift worth memorializing.

We found the life He had in store for us because we followed His way. And whether or not you can claim that for your deceased loved one, I pray that you can make that your reality—for yourself and for the rest of those you love.

If you are not already following Jesus Christ, know that He has a better life for you. You only need to find this life in Him so that your existence can someday be memorialized as a life that was lived on earth but worthy of all of heaven's rewards.

WORKBOOK

Chapter Four Reflection

Prompt: In a journal or notebook, write down a memory of a loved one who is no longer with you. Choose a memory that brings you comfort and happiness to remember. And if you haven't already, come up with a long-lasting memorial you can create to remember your loved one always.

CHAPTER FIVE

Faith for the Journey

Victory is obtained the moment we proclaim fellowship with God and walk with Him on the path He has forged for us. It's a victory in that moment because you will immediately experience the peace that comes with reliance on God. It's also a victory for eternity because by walking with Him, you are guaranteeing yourself a life in heaven for all time.

Choosing to walk in victory with God isn't always easy, especially in challenging times. Whether you've lost someone close to you or you're struggling through any number of things happening in the world right now, the key to walking in victory is having faith on your journey.

Faith isn't just an abstract concept. It's not about demanding proof before you move forward. Faith is unchangeable. It's constant and immovable.

Faith is something you stand in with integrity, that cannot be moved no matter what conflict is swirling around you. Faith is hope; it's a steadfast belief in something you cannot see, and it's always there—even though it may be more difficult to hold onto in challenging times.

Faith is one of the most powerful forces in our lives. It's so powerful that without it, you will not complete this journey in victory.

The Journey

Put simply, the word *journey* means the "act of traveling from one place to another."[9] But there's a more specific definition I want to focus on. It also means, "A long and often difficult process of personal change and development."[10]

So, this journey we're on is a metaphor for a long period of travel, but it also accurately describes what you're going through on an emotional level. As you move forward in faith, you will continue to change and develop into a person who is prepared for the next stage in this life God has mapped out for you.

I understand that this might be hard to accept right now. Maybe you don't want to change. Maybe everything seemed perfect before you lost your loved one, or perhaps you spend every waking moment wishing you could go back to the time before their passing.

You might want to reject any notion of embracing change because, you reason, there was nothing wrong with your life before this event. But remember, no matter what you had in the past, God is trying to bring forth a better "you" for your future.

That's why you need faith. You can't see what lies ahead. The only way to move forward, and through this grief, is to trust (have faith) in God, understanding that He is all-knowing and has your best interest as His first priority.

Faith is an assurance of things to come, as we're guaranteed in Hebrews: "Now faith is the substance of things hoped for, the evidence of things not seen" (Hebrews 11:1). This means that faith will carry you through your present state with a confident belief about your future.

Please know that there are still some good things up ahead for you.

Faith Is Your Travel Companion

There are few things that can give you confidence without being seen, but faith is one of those things. It's a phenomenon, really. By trusting in something you can't see, you are better equipped to travel along a road you can't see—and believe me when I say that *it will always work out*.

How do I know that? Faith.

I know that no matter how demanding the journey becomes, victory always awaits. Even through trials that seem unbearable, faith is victorious.

I know you can't see it right now, and neither can I. But faith provides confidence in what is to come. Faith tells us there are blessings ahead we cannot predict and that we are not even able to imagine right now.

Earlier, I talked about a journey being a process of personal change and development. That means the person you will become, on the other side of your journey, will be capable of accepting those things that don't seem possible to you right now.

So, confidence in your future means knowing that you will not go into victory feeling the way you do now. This is a temporary state. The intensity of grief you're feeling will not accompany you for the rest of your days—if, that is, you're willing to give navigation of this journey over to God.

When the children of Israel found themselves wandering in the wilderness, they struggled to have hope for their future. That's because they didn't have faith. The Lord was bringing about personal change and development for each one of them individually and for them all as a people. He was taking them on a journey, both literal and figurative. Many of them didn't get to experience what He had in store for them because they did not have faith in Him. This should serve as a stark example for every one of us about how important faith is.

Things We Can Be Sure Of

Faith is the assurance of things to come, but that doesn't mean we won't see evidence of the Lord as we move along this journey.

1. He will bring us through this. "For His anger endureth but a moment; in His favor is life: weeping may endure for a night, but joy cometh in the morning" (Psalm 30:5). I am reminded of something that was given to my wife from the Lord at a critical time in her life. She had been betrayed by some individuals whom she loved and trusted. God told her that she would be able to live, laugh, and love again. He assured her that she would get through it, and it came to pass. He will do the same for you.

2. Despite what has happened, God will still accomplish His purpose in your life. His divine intention has not vanished. It is still the reason for your existence. It's not over for you. His plan and purpose for your life are still in motion.

3. God has many promises in store for us—many of them too magnificent for us to envision. "And we desire that every one of you do shew the same diligence to the full assurance of hope unto the end: that ye be not slothful, but followers of them who through faith and patience inherit the promises" (Hebrews 6:11–12). And if we need more than that, we can look to Joshua: "Moses my servant is dead; now therefore arise, go over this Jordan, thou, and all this people, unto the land which I do give to them, even to the children of Israel. Every place that the sole of your foot shall tread upon, that have I given unto you, as I said unto Moses. From the wilderness and this Lebanon even unto the great river, the river Euphrates, all the land of the Hittites, and unto the great sea toward the going down of the sun, shall be your coast" (Joshua 1:2–4). The Lord is not through with blessing you yet.

As you move through this journey in victory and toward victory, pay attention to those things that God makes evident along the way. These are sign posts meant to strengthen our faith and relationship with the Lord. Acknowledge and give Him all the credit, knowing that all good things come through Him.

So Much More to Come

Even if it doesn't feel like it right now, you have so much more to live for. You don't need to predict what's ahead. You don't have to map it out. All you need is faith.

I know, that can be easier said than done.

As you move toward owning the faith necessary for the journey, keep this passage close to you: "So then faith cometh by hearing, and hearing by the Word of God" (Romans 10:17). This means you only need to keep your heart open to the Lord. He will speak to you. He will give you the direction you need to stay on the path. You only need to stay plugged into Him, your source for all things.

At this time, when it's most tempting to live your life void of His Word, remember that His Word is necessary to sustain faith. "But He answered and said, It is written, Man shall not live by bread alone, but by every word that proceedeth out of the mouth of God" (Matthew 4:4).

The Enemy's Intentions

> *But without faith it is impossible to please Him: for he that cometh to God must believe that he is, and that He is a rewarder of them that diligently seek Him.*
> **—Hebrews 11:6**

Satan, the enemy, knows that without faith, we cannot complete this journey. Therefore, his ultimate goal is to wreck our faith so that we cannot be victorious with God. This is his victory.

And while the enemy is tempting you to abandon your

faith, I am encouraging you to hold onto it. Hold onto it with everything you have, because it's the key to getting you through to the other side.

I know how difficult it can be—I have my moments, every day. But along with every one of those moments comes my faith, which keeps those moments from turning into hours, days, and years.

The Lord Is with You

There's reason for you to have faith in your future. I can share this because I know all things will be well with my future, even though my life partner has gone on to be with the Lord.

With that same faith, you can have confidence in what's next for you. That reason is the Lord. More specifically, that reason is because *the Lord is with you.*

> *He has always been there, has never left, and will never leave. Let your conversation be without covetousness; and be content with such things as ye have: for he hath said, I will never leave thee, nor forsake thee. So that we may boldly say, The Lord is my helper, and I will not fear what man shall do unto me.*
> —**Hebrews 13:5-6**

Joseph was able to testify of what the Lord had in store for him on his journey. He experienced some very dark times. He was sold into slavery and betrayed by his brethren.

> *And Joseph was brought down to Egypt; and Potiphar, an officer of Pharaoh, captain of the guard, an Egyptian, bought him of the hands of the Ishmeelites, which had brought him down thither. And the LORD was with Joseph, and he was a prosperous man; and he was in the house of his master the Egyptian. And his master saw that the LORD was with him, and that the LORD made all that he did to prosper in his hand. And Joseph found grace in his sight, and he served him: and he made him overseer over his house, and all that he had he put into his hand.*
> **—Genesis 39:1–4**

Through it all, the Lord was with Joseph. And look at what the Lord did:

> *And Joseph's master took him, and put him into the prison, a place where the king's prisoners were bound: and he was there in the prison. But the LORD was with Joseph, and shewed him mercy, and gave him favour in the sight of the keeper of the prison. And the keeper of the prison committed to Joseph's hand all the prisoners that were in the prison; and whatsoever they did there, he was the doer of it. The keeper of the prison looked not to any thing that was under his hand; because the LORD was with him, and that which he did, the LORD made it to prosper.*
> **—Genesis 39:20–23**

The Lord is also with you. Even now. Especially now.

The Lord reaffirms His covenant to His people: "Fear thou not; for I am with thee: be not dismayed; for I am thy God: I will strengthen thee; yea, I will help thee; yea, I will uphold thee with the right hand of my righteousness" (Isaiah 41:10).

He asks us not to be dismayed, which is the complete breakdown of courage. Being dismayed means becoming disheartened, losing determination, failing in confidence, losing hope, and being discouraged. He does not want this for us. Instead, He wants us to trust in his wisdom, power, and concern for us.

> *God is our refuge and strength, a very present help in trouble. Therefore will not we fear, though the earth be removed, and though the mountains be carried into the midst of the sea; though the waters thereof roar and be troubled, though the mountains shake with the swelling thereof. Selah. There is a river, the streams whereof shall make glad the city of God, the holy place of the tabernacles of the most High. God is in the midst of her; she shall not be moved: God shall help her, and that right early.*
> **—Psalms 46:1–5**

God is not only with you, alongside you. He is also *for* you. He's on your side and wants nothing more than for you to be triumphant: "What shall we then say to these things? If God be for us, who can be against us?" (Romans 8:31).

I know this is hard, but if you do nothing else, be steadfast in faith. That alone will bring you through. You see, faith speaks for what is to come. It has a voice, if only we silence our hearts to listen.

As you take God's hand in faith, you will want to speak for what is to come. The only way to do that is to attach your faith to the only One who can determine what that is. Jesus tells us how in the Gospel of Mark:

> *And Jesus answering saith unto them, Have faith in God.*

> *For verily I say unto you, That whosoever shall say unto this mountain, Be thou removed, and be thou cast into the sea; and shall not doubt in his heart, but shall believe that those things which he saith shall come to pass; he shall have whatsoever he saith. Therefore I say unto you, What things soever ye desire, when ye pray, believe that ye receive them, and ye shall have them. And when ye stand praying, forgive, if ye have ought against any: that your Father also which is in heaven may forgive you your trespasses.*
>
> **—Mark 11:22–25**

That, my friend, is the path to victory.

WORKBOOK

Chapter Five Reflection

Question: In a journal or notebooks, reflect on the ways God has shown Himself faithful in your life.

CHAPTER SIX

Bitter or Better?

The final leg of your journey through grief may be the most significant. You will come to a fork in the road. You can choose to put everything you've endured so far to good use as part of God's plan. Or you can choose to live in the past, holding onto your anger, fear, and resentment. At this junction, one choice will lead you to a joyful life. The other will lead to a dead end—or worse, it will dump you into a deep, dark pit that will be difficult to escape.

If you have traveled with God and opened your heart to His Word, you know that He won't abandon you at this critical junction. He knows you have this choice to make. When you arrive and stare down those two divergent paths, He will be with you to point you toward the way that will lead to a triumphant life—the path that will give birth to beauty out of your grief.

The Journey Toward Change

As I move through my own grief, I have been presented with a question: *"Am I going to become bitter, or will I get better?"*

The Lord does not wish for us to grow in bitterness toward Him or toward the life He has prescribed for us. Remember that the word *journey* means a long and often difficult process of personal change and development. Your journey is proof that the Lord wants to see you change and develop into someone who is prepared for the next part of your life.

As you may already know, change isn't something that just happens. Many times, change happens when we are faced with an unescapable choice. In other words, you can change or you can be miserable for the rest of your life.

The biggest changes happen when we're faced with having to navigate through great pain. The greater the pain, the more likely you are to change. Oftentimes, the extraordinary life events that cause change—like what you and I are faced with—are necessary for that change to happen.

Say Yes to Change

The word *change* means to make or become different.[11] I like to define it as "to transform or to become a different person entirely."

Change can speak to someone's attitude or their behavior. It can refer to a shift in someone's outlook on life or the way in which they treat themselves and others. It can take on the form of a physical alteration, as with weight loss. Or it can be psychological, emotional, and spiritual. In many cases, it covers all of the above.

The moment you realize something about you needs to change—whether that's one hundred percent internal or in response to an outside stimulus or event—that's when the change begins to take place. That's the acknowledgement of something having to give way for something new. It's the acceptance of whatever has happened (knowing you can't erase that) and moving ahead with the only thing you have control over—your own thoughts and actions.

Some of that change will be in your hands. It will be a choice you make. And when you make that choice, you will feel the Lord working through you to complete the change that's necessary for moving forward along the path of life He has forged for you.

In many ways, the biggest barrier to successful change is the word *no*. Even if you're not consciously saying no to God, you are blocking the change He wants for you by not saying yes to Him.

So pay attention to what the Lord is trying to change in you at this time. It's easy to get wrapped up in the pain, but when you look ahead and ask, "Where's the lesson in this?" you will move through the grief more triumphantly. You will make a change that benefits you and others, and you will deepen your relationship with God.

The changes God is making in you will lead you closer to His heart and a few steps closer to the "greater" God has for you. These changes, although they may not always be desirable, will bring growth and development leading toward the ultimate victory you will have in Christ as you walk with Him. All God is looking for is your *yes*—so He can lead you into victory.

Develop Toward Victory

The word *development* means "a process that creates growth, progress, or positive change."[12] Take note, that's *positive* change—not negative. The Lord would not enact these events in your life intending for you to spiral or turn toward darkness and evil.

Development speaks to your capabilities. It uses the gifts, talents, and passions that were born with you and nurtures them so they'll be ready to share with the world, to enact positive change in others' lives.

As you move through this, it's crucial that you pay attention to the pieces of you that the Lord awakens and brings to the forefront. These are the things He wants to develop in you, and He needs your cooperation to make it happen.

If you allow Him to have His way, the end result will be a happier, more fulfilled you. You will discover things about yourself you never knew. You will summon the courage to do the things you were once afraid to do. You are forged in fire because you made it through this grief, and you will eventually realize that without this pain, the development you and everyone around you values so highly would not have taken place.

When you have completed this phase of your earthly development, you will be able to look back at the person you were and appreciate the road you traveled. You are not a bad person now, by any means. However, you will be better when you arrive at victory.

Better, Not Bitter

And there it is: when you have gone through the change and development that's waiting for you, you will be a *better* person. You will not be bitter. You will have the hindsight that's essential for seeing that things unfolded just as they had to—because those events all tied into God's plan.

In every stage and aspect of life, God is guiding you toward being a better person. The only way you'll end up bitter is if you resist His guidance.

A bitter person is filled with anger and resentment. They are unhappy because they cannot accept the things that have happened in their past. Because of this, they possess an unpleasant attitude. They become harsh in their dealings with others. Ecclesiastes says, "Be not hasty in thy spirit to be angry: for anger resteth in the bosom of fool" (Ecclesiastes 7:9).

When the anger stage of grief is held onto—without the acceptance of the event or of the change that is inevitable—then bitterness is given space to move in. It can last for a lifetime. It saturates every area of life, crippling your ability to experience joy. A bitter life is a miserable one, and innocent people will suffer because of it. The Bible says, "And another dieth in the bitterness of his soul, and never eateth with pleasure" (Job 21:25).

Bitterness can defile an otherwise sparkling soul, causing it to become soiled and to lose its purity. It can turn a good person into a bad one—and I know you don't want that to happen to you. So, as we learn in Ephesians, we have to get rid of it: "Let all bitterness, and wrath, and anger, and clamour, and evil speaking, be put away from you, with all malice" (Ephesians 4:31).

The New-and-Improved You

The Lord is working right now. He's producing a better you than you've ever known. He's improving you, and you're going to feel some growing pains. He wants you to be you, to the fullest. He wants you to live a fulfilling life, and He wants you to have a great impact on the lives of others.

As you transform through the pain of grief, and as you get better, I encourage you to feel your emotions—feel them deeply—and then move forward. Do not let anger or sorrow overtake you. Do not allow them to turn into bitterness or depression that can pull you down and keep you from being the person God created you to be.

And with that, I would like to leave you with these two scriptures, from Genesis and 1 Samuel, which relate to two individuals who allowed themselves to become better instead of bitter. Their decisions to become better ultimately resulted in them becoming who God called them to be:

> *And Jacob was left alone; and there wrestled a man with him until the breaking of the day. And when he saw that he prevailed not against him, he touched the hollow of his thigh; and the hollow of Jacob's thigh was out of joint, as he wrestled with him. And he said, Let me go, for the day breaketh. And he said, I will not let thee go, except thou*

bless me. And he said unto him, What is thy name? And he said, Jacob. And he said, Thy name shall be called no more Jacob, but Israel: for as a prince hast thou power with God and with men, and hast prevailed. And Jacob asked him, and said, Tell me, I pray thee, thy name. And he said, Wherefore is it that thou dost ask after my name? And he blessed him there. And Jacob called the name of the place Peniel: for I have seen God face to face, and my life is preserved.
—Genesis 32:24–30

*Moreover, my father, see, yea, see the skirt of thy robe in my hand: for in that I cut off the skirt of thy robe, and killed thee not, know thou and see that there is neither evil nor transgression in mine hand, and I have not sinned against thee; yet thou huntest my soul to take it. The L*ORD* judge between me and thee, and the L*ORD* avenge me of thee: but mine hand shall not be upon thee. As saith the proverb of the ancients, Wickedness proceedeth from the wicked: but mine hand shall not be upon thee. After whom is the king of Israel come out? after whom dost thou pursue? after a dead dog, after a flea. The L*ORD* therefore be judge, and judge between me and thee, and see, and plead my cause, and deliver me out of thine hand. And it came to pass, when David had made an end of speaking these words unto Saul, that Saul said, Is this thy voice, my son David? And Saul lifted up his voice, and wept. And he said to David, Thou art more righteous than I: for thou hast rewarded me good, whereas I have rewarded thee evil. And thou hast shewed this day how that thou hast dealt well with me: forasmuch as when the L*ORD* had delivered me into thine hand, thou killedst me not. For if a man find his enemy, will he let him go well away? wherefore the L*ORD* reward thee good for that thou hast done unto me this day. And now, behold, I know well that thou shalt surely be king, and that the kingdom of Israel shall be established in thine hand.*
—1 Samuel 24:11–20

Always remember that Jacob became Israel and David became king. You, too, shall journey to becoming someone better than you ever could have been without this experience. You are predestined to fill a particular role, for a particular purpose. Qualities are being developed within you that will fulfill that destiny.

All you have to do is take God's hand. Walk with Him through this, to the promised land.

WORKBOOK

Chapter Six Reflection

Question: In a notebook or journal, write honestly the aspects of this journey which have tempted you to become bitter. As a contrast, write the ways you have seen God growing you and making you a better person through this process of grief.

CONCLUSION

You Can Do This

Those things, which ye have both learned, and received, and heard, and seen in me, do: and the God of peace shall be with you.

But I rejoiced in the Lord greatly, that now at the last your care of me hath flourished again; wherein ye were also careful, but ye lacked opportunity.

Not that I speak in respect of want: for I have learned, in whatsoever state I am, therewith to be content.

I know how to be abased, and I know how to abound: every where and in all things I am instructed both to be full and to be hungry, both to abound and to suffer need.

I can do all things through Christ which strengtheneth me.
—**Philippians 4:9–13**

Paul lived what he preached. His life actually spoke more eloquently than his lips. Like the saying goes, his actions spoke louder than words. This is why Paul had the authority to reassure the Philippian believers that God would be with them in the most turbulent of times.

You Can Be Content

Even when it seems the world has turned upside-down, God will be with you. This is why Paul found satisfaction and happiness in whatever state he was in, no matter the state of the circumstances he was in. God has a way of breathing contentment into His people.

In the lowest and highest places of your life, you can also find contentment. When God is with you and on your side, you can find a sense of rest and peace no matter what.

In all things, you can continue to be strengthened by the One who infuses you with His power. God is with you in the valley and on the mountaintop. He provides the strength you need to make it through any situation or circumstance you may face in life.

You Are an Overcomer

It's hard for you to overcome in a particular area of your life when you are convinced you are not able. Think about things you couldn't do in the past. Once you realized you could do it, you did! No matter what you are dealing with, you can declare over your life and circumstances, "I can do this."

First Corinthians 10:13 says, "There hath no temptation taken you but such as is common to man: but God is faithful, who will not suffer you to be tempted above that ye are able; but will with the temptation also make a way to escape, that ye may be able to bear it." It's all about having the right mindset. This is the key.

He knows exactly what you can handle. Why would you be faced with something you can't overcome? God won't allow that to happen to you!

First John 4:4 says, "Ye are of God, little children, and have overcome them: because greater is he that is in you, than he that is in the world." Let it sink in—you are a child of God! You belong to Him! You have a greater One on the inside of you, and you are never alone.

You Have the Victory

Who shall separate us from the love of Christ? Shall tribulation, or distress, or persecution, or famine, or nakedness, or peril, or sword?

As it is written, For thy sake we are killed all the day long; we are accounted as sheep for the slaughter.

Nay, in all these things we are more than conquerors through him that loved us.

For I am persuaded, that neither death, nor life, nor angels, nor principalities, nor powers, nor things present, nor things to come, nor height, nor depth, nor any other creature, shall be able to separate us from the love of God, which is in Christ Jesus our Lord.
—Romans 8:35-39

God's love is still working in the midst of difficult times. You may not be exempt from trials and tribulations, but His love conquers all. It doesn't matter who doesn't like you. It just matters that you remember the One who loves you. It doesn't matter who turns their back on you. It matters that the One who created you is standing up on your behalf.

God knows how to take care of His own. He fed His people in the wilderness. He will also take care of you, because He loves you!

Second Corinthians 2:14 says, "Now thanks be unto God, which always causeth us to triumph in Christ, and maketh manifest the savour of his knowledge by us in every place." *Always!* In every situation, He has already given you the victory. This is why I know you can do anything—because you already have the victory.

First John 5:4–5 says, "For whatsoever is born of God overcometh the world: and this is the victory that overcometh the world, even our faith. Who is he that overcometh the world, but he that believeth that Jesus is the Son of God?" Because you are born again and a child of God, you've already been destined to overcome anything that may come your way.

It's up to you to release faith upon the truths in God's Word and have a shift in your mind. Settle in your heart that no matter what unexpected journey God has you on, He will lead you through to victory.

A Tribute to My Wife
Robbin Eames Hardy

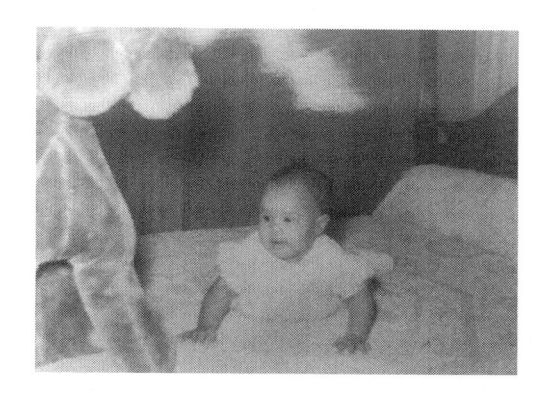

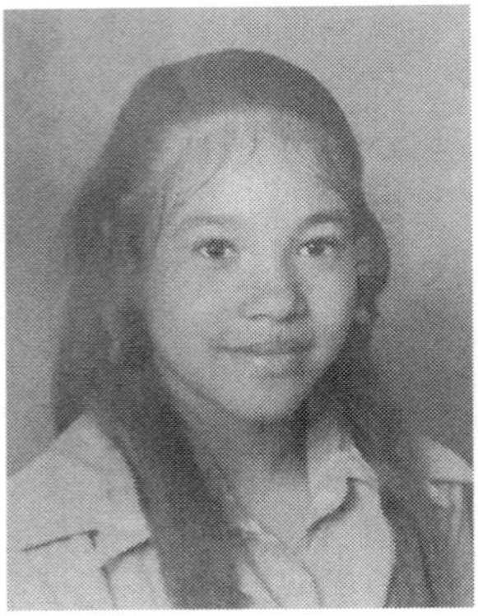

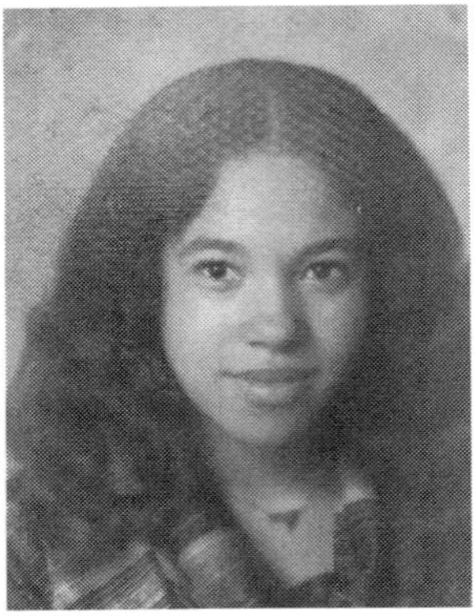

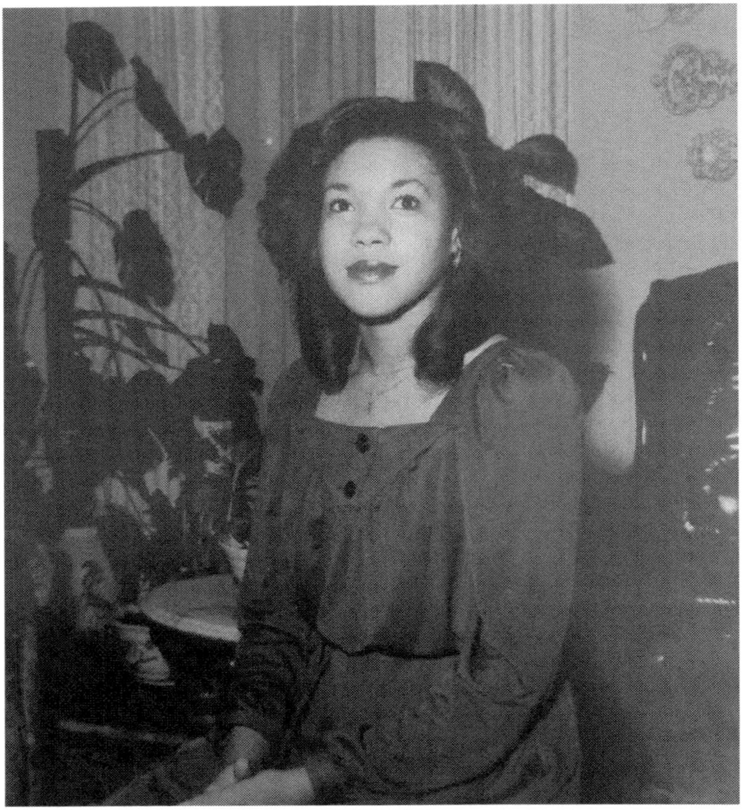

THE UNEXPECTED JOURNEY · 83

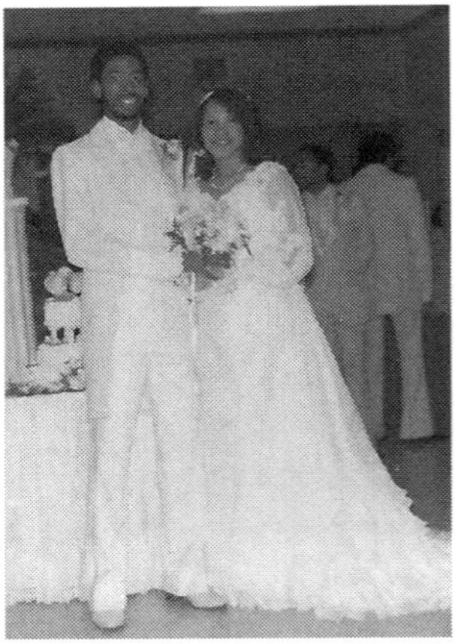

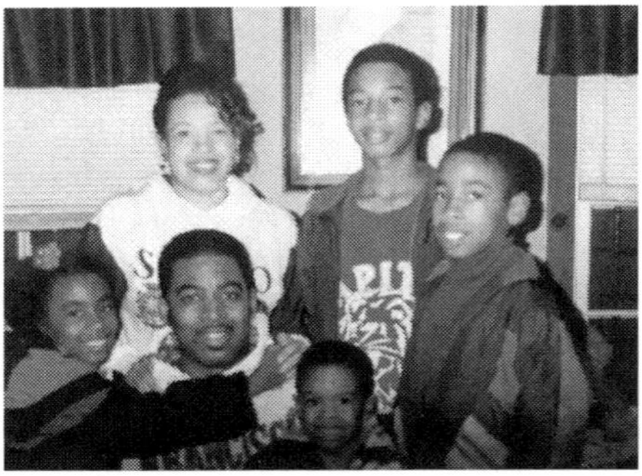

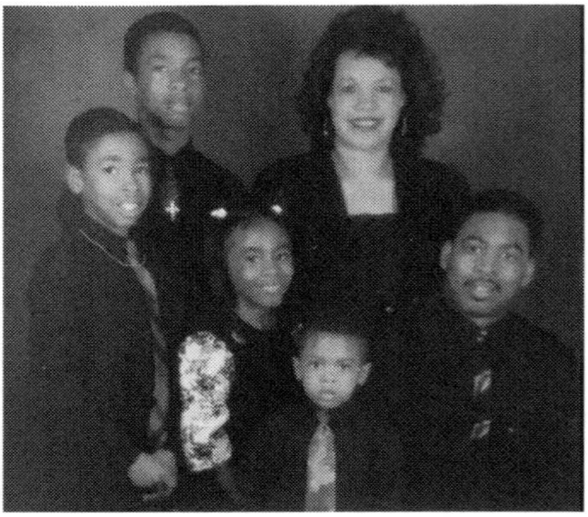

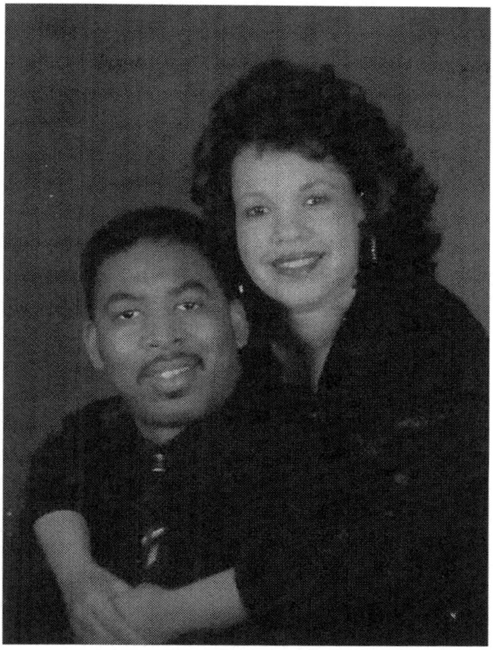

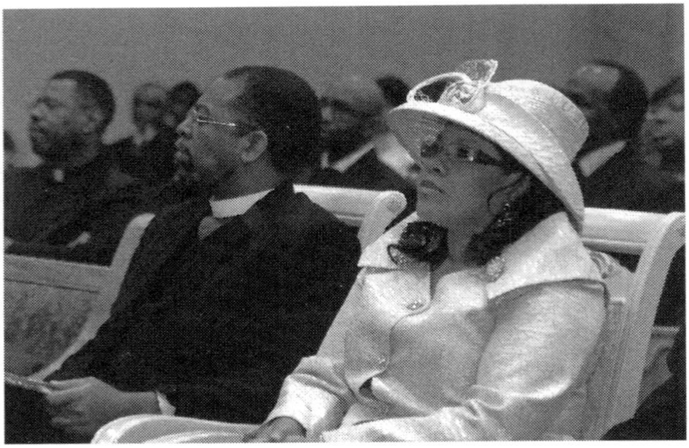

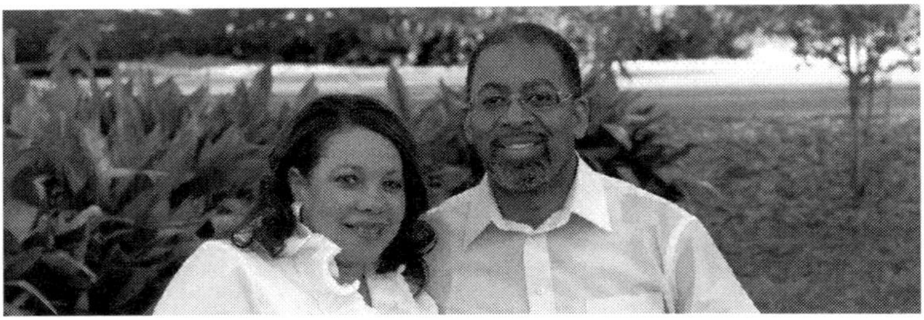

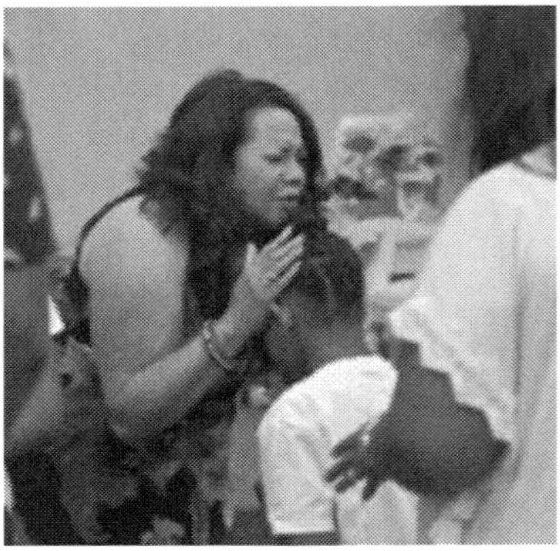

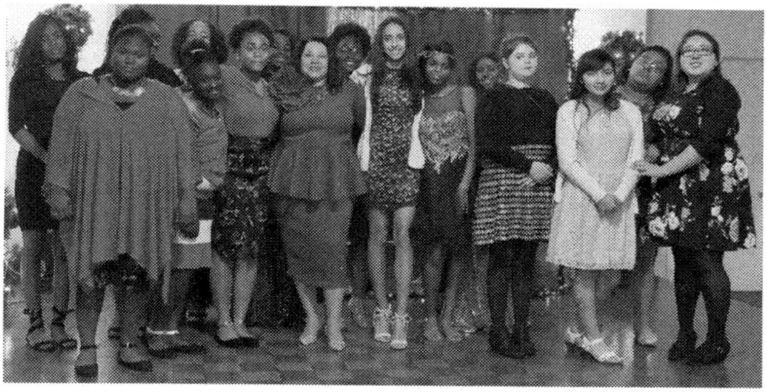

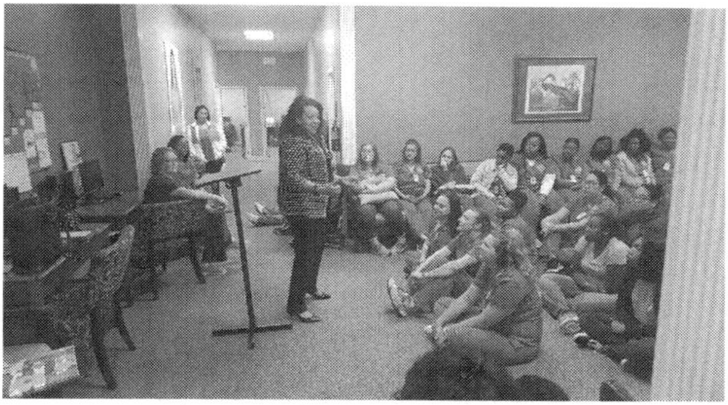

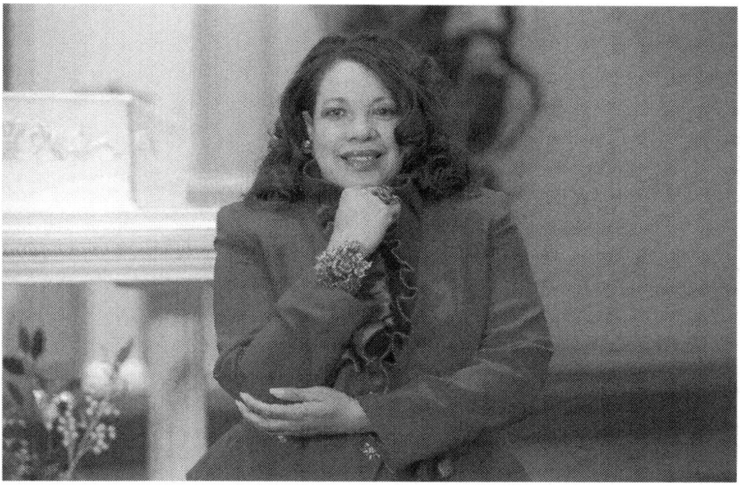

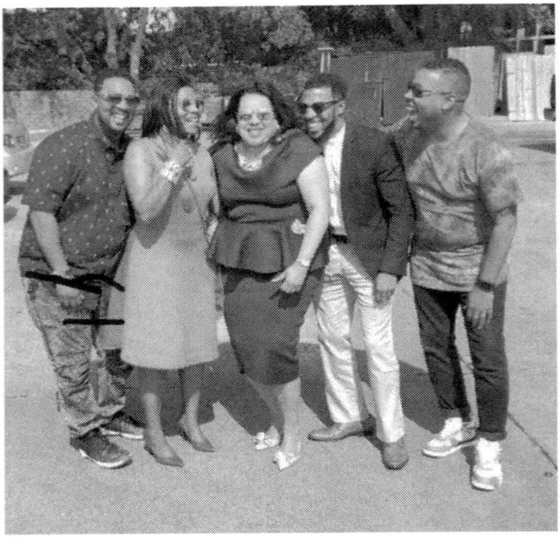

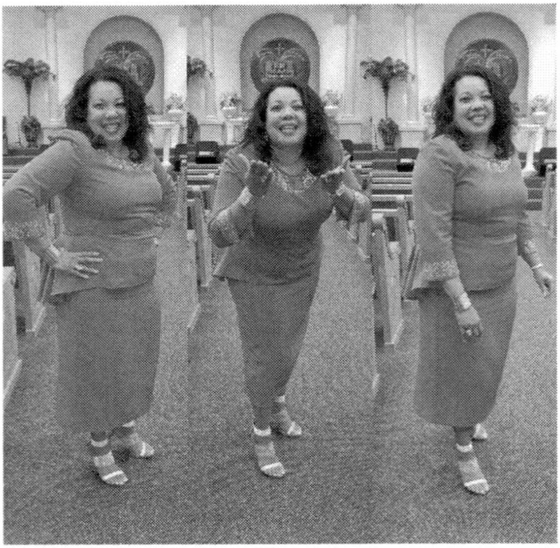

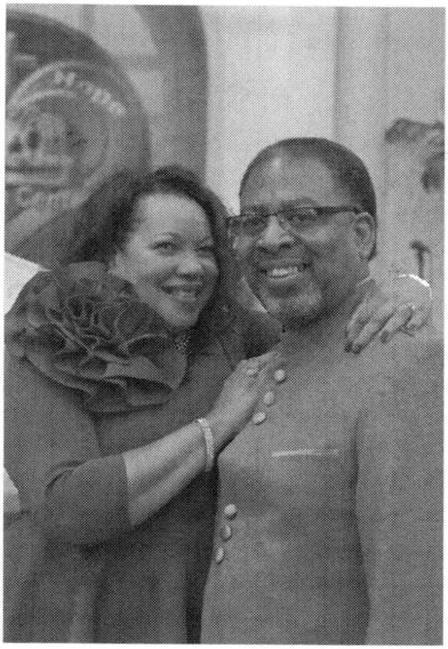

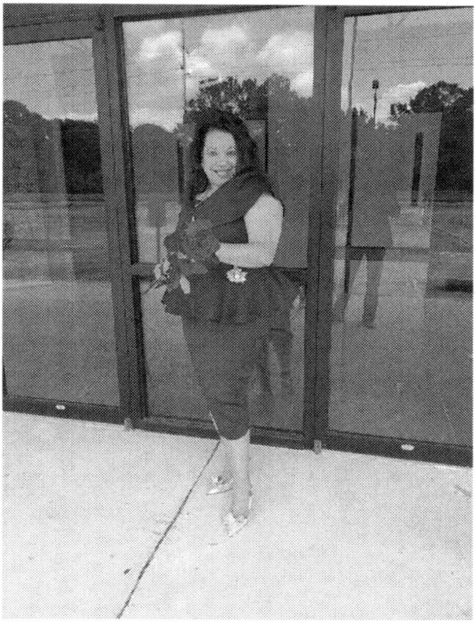

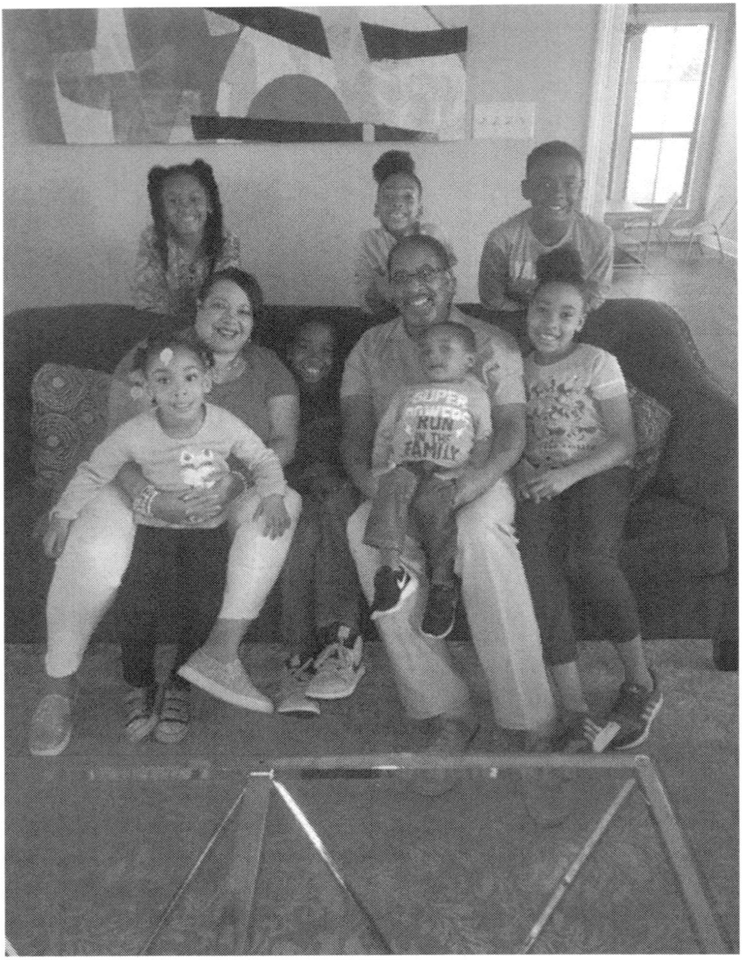
SUPER
POWERS
RUN
FAMILY

REFERENCES

Notes

1. Hillsong United. "Oceans (Where Feet May Fail)." Track 4 on *Zion*. Capitol Christian Music Group, 2013.

2. Jakes, T. D. "TD Jakes – Leading While Bleeding 2004 Part 3. YouTube video. March 24, 2014. https://www.youtube.com/watch?v=6Lnrhy0VPKM.

3. *Lexico,* "grief." https://www.lexico.com/en/definition/grief.

4. *Lexico,* "keep." https://www.lexico.com/definition/keep.

5. *Lexico,* "trust." https://www.lexico.com/definition/trust.

6. Raymond, Jon. "Knowing What You Don't Know." Huffpost. May 25, 2011. https://www.huffpost.com/entry/knowing-what-you-dont-kno_b_132846?guccounter=1.

7. *Lexico,* "blessed." https://www.lexico.com/definition/blessed.

8. *Dictionary.com,* "blessed." https://www.dictionary.com/browse/blessed.

9. *Lexico,* "journey." https://www.lexico.com/definition/journey.

10. *Lexico,* "journey."

11. *Lexico,* "change." https://www.lexico.com/definition/change.

12. Sid Israel. "What Is Development?" Society for International Development Israel Branch. March 11, 2018. https:// www.sid-israel.org/en/Development-Issues/What-is-Development#:~:text=Development%20is%20a%20process%20that,environmental%2C%20social%20and%20demographic%20components.

About the Author

Ronald Hardy, Sr. is the fifth of six children, born to the late Willie Hardy, Jr. and Yvonne Hardy. At the age of nineteen, Ronald gave his life to the Lord. Less than one year later, he married the woman of his dreams, the late Robbin Eames Hardy. To this union, five children were born, one deceased. The family has continued to expand, and now Ronald is also the proud grandfather of seven grandchildren.

At the age of twenty-seven, Ronald stepped into his purpose when he became the pastor of Faith, Hope and Love Fellowship, currently known as Faith, Hope and Love Worship Center. Thirteen years later, he launched a second location of Faith, Hope and Love Worship Center, and the ministry became "one church in two locations." After serving as a pastor for more than nineteen years, Ronald was installed as a bishop, a title that he currently holds.

Throughout their thirty-eight years of marriage, Ronald and his wife, Robbin, worked together to launch their own business, host marriage seminars and retreats, and co-author a book entitled, *A Love Like This*. They also partnered together to found two organizations: G.E.M.S. (Girls Enrichment Mentorship Services) and F.L.I.P. (Fatherless Leaders Initiative Program). Both organizations were instrumental in reaching students in the West Feliciana and East Baton Rouge school systems.

Ronald is an author, teacher, and prophet, and a Licensed Certified Grief Coach. His passion is to help people embrace the fulness of all the Lord has in store for them.

Contact info for Ronald is below.

Phone number: 225-287-9113

Email address: ronaldhardysr61@gmail.com

Facebook: https://www.facebook.com/bishopronaldhardysr/

One of the most important lessons I've learned is that you cannot go through grief alone. You need your family, friends, and God to help you navigate the process of grief.

This is what motivated me to become a licensed grief coach, working 1-on-1 or in small groups to help guide those suffering with grief. I walk with those on the journey of grief, hand in hand with God, to help you and your family find a way past the suffering and onto a path of value and purpose.

You can schedule a FREE 30-minute call with me, and just for talking with me, you'll also receive a free copy of my book: The Unexpected Journey (while supply lasts).

Visit https://links.ronaldhardygriefbook.com/call to schedule your call.

About Renown Publishing

Renown Publishing was founded with one mission in mind: to make your great idea famous.

At Renown Publishing, we don't just publish. We work hard to pair strategy with innovative marketing techniques so that your book launch is the start of something bigger.

Learn more at RenownPublishing.com.

Made in the USA
Columbia, SC
07 May 2023